Farm Smart Kids

Volume #1

Equine Colors

Beth McCollum

FARM SMART KIDS: EQUINE COLORS by Beth McCollum
Volume #1

Copyright©2015 by Beth McCollum

Photographs by Beth McCollum

Book design and interior layout by Ellie Searl, Publishista®

ISBN-10: 0692434526
ISBN-13: 9780692434529

All rights reserved. No part of this publication may be reproduced, distributed, or transmitted in any form or by any means, including photocopying, recording, or other electronic or mechanical methods, without the prior written permission of the publisher, except in the case of brief quotations embodied in critical reviews and certain other noncommercial uses permitted by copyright law.

GYPSY DREAM PUBLISHING
Batesville, AR

This book is dedicated to every American cowboy and cowgirl.

Thank you for all your hard work in keeping alive the History, Tradition, and Legacy of Rodeo in America.

Beth McCollum

Horses come in **many colors.**

**White,
gray,
and
black . . .**

. . . are just a few.

Let's visit the rodeo,

and see if you can learn more
about horse colors.

Buckskin is what you call a horse

with a tan or
golden coat,

black mane, tail,
and lower legs.

Now it's your turn.

Which horse

is a

buckskin?

A Palomino

has a
golden coat,

and the mane
and tail are
white.

A sorrel horse

has a reddish colored body

with the same color or lighter mane and tail.

Now it's your turn.

Which horse

is a
sorrel?

[If you said the one on the left, you are correct.]

Look at these horses.

Can you tell their colors

all by yourself?

A bay horse

has a reddish-brown coat

with black mane, tail, lower legs, and ear edges.

This horse is called a dun.

See the dark stripe down the center of the back?

It's a gene that affects both red and black pigments in the coat colors.

Look closely

at these
two horses.

Which one is
the dun?

16

These are **paint** colored horses,

and no two
are just alike.

Sometimes they
are called a
pinto,

depending on their bloodlines.

Natural **paint** markings must be a certain size,

and be on certain parts of the body to be registered as a **paint.**

One horse
is not like the others.

Can you tell
which horse is
not a
paint?

You are doing great!

Now look closely, and try again.

One horse is a paint

and the other is a palomino.

These are called **roan** horses.

Roan horses

have white hairs mixed in with the
other colored hairs.

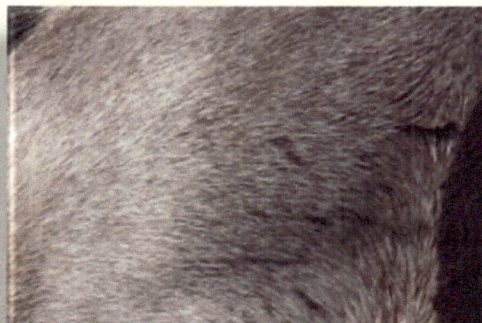

The appaloosa

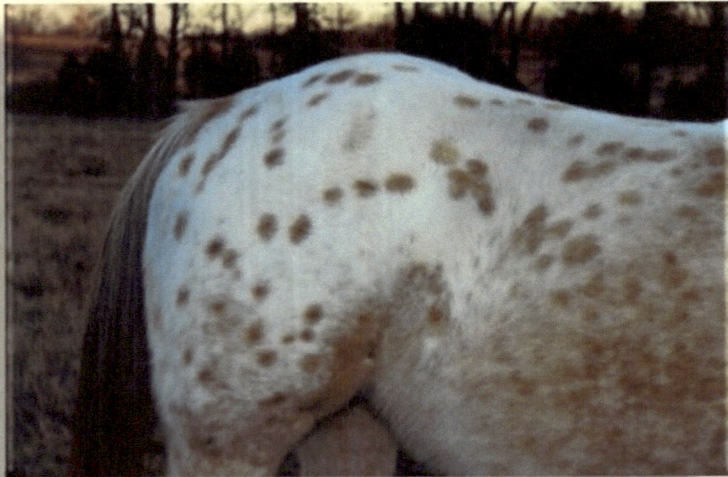

has
colorful spots.

A closer look shows an **appaloosa's** hooves have stripes.

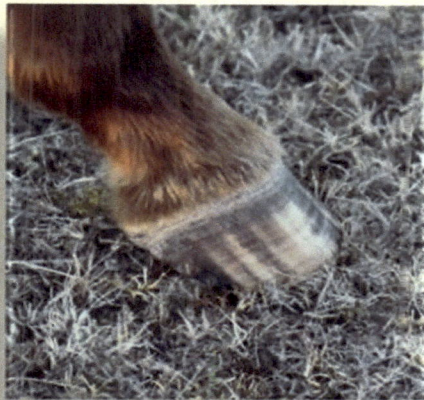

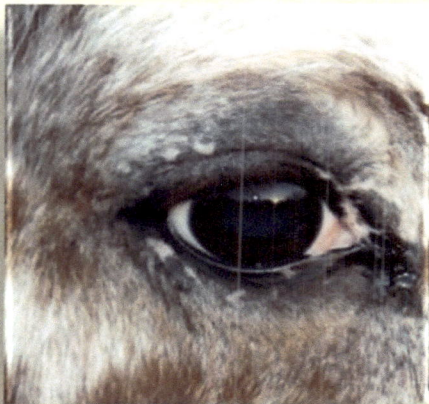

Also you can see the white around an **appaloosa's** eyes easier than on most other horses.

Let's recap the new colors you have learned
at the rodeo.
They are:

Buckskin

Palomino

Sorrel

Bay

Dun

Paint

Roan

Appaloosa

25

Join me again soon for

another lesson about

FARM SMART KIDS.

www.ingramcontent.com/pod-product-compliance
Lightning Source LLC
Chambersburg PA
CBHW042117040426
42449CB00002B/77